Decentralized Social Media

The Future of Online Communication and Blockchain

Table of Contents

Chapter 1. Introduction

The dawn of online communication is evolving, shifting the paradigm towards a new horizon - Decentralized Social Media. This highly engaging and thought-provoking Special Report dives deep into this burgeoning technology, demonstrating how the fusion of blockchain implementations can revolutionize our current understanding of social platforms. While the discussion delves into complex, technical elements, it is neatly broken down into digestible lessons. Irrespective of your level of technical savvy, you will find yourself navigating through the intricacies of decentralized systems, cryptography, and consensus algorithms, with newfound clarity. This report promises not just knowledge, but a panoramic perspective on how future online communication could shape society, economies, and individual freedoms with unwavering precision. Like standing at the brink of a new universe ready to be discovered, this Special Report draws you in, beckoning you to leap into the intriguing world of Decentralized Social Media. Start the journey – because the future of online communication is just a page away.

Chapter 2. Understanding Traditional Social Media: A Primer

Understanding the fundamental principles and workings of traditional social media is integral to appreciating its evolution into its imminent future: the blockchain-driven, decentralized alternative. This chapter acts as a preparatory course, focusing on building the foundations that will enable us to proceed further into an exciting new realm of communication.

2.1. History of Social Media

A quick retrospective glance is necessary to comprehend the inception and subsequent growth of social media. In essence, social media, is an offshoot of the human desire to communicate. From hieroglyphics to handwritten letters and telegrams, each mode of communication sought to reduce spatial constraints and boost interactivity.

In the late 1970s, computers sparked a breakthrough. Bulletin Board Systems allowed for unprecedented user-generated content sharing and discussions, establishing the foundation for subsequent internet-based communication and the birth of social media.

Websites like SixDegrees.com arrived in 1997, which allowed users to create profiles and friend others. Fast forward to the 2000s, and platforms like Friendster, MySpace, and most crucially Facebook, propelled social media into global consciousness.

In the present, social media has evolved into a ubiquitous aspect of life, seeping into politics, business, entertainment, and community building. Though draped in different interfaces and gimmicks, the core model of connecting human experiences remains constant.

2.2. Social Media and User Interaction

At the core of every social media platform lies user interaction. User generated content, whether expressed as likes, shares, retweets, or comments, drive these platforms forward, ensuring their continuous relevance and appeal.

Traditional social media allows the user to share everything, from daily life snippets to professional achievements, opinions, ideas, and queries. The essence of social media lies in its capability to collapse geographical barriers and facilitate real-time engagement among the global populace.

Platforms such as Instagram or TikTok have even honed an innovative consumption format. They employ a highly visual, algorithm-driven delivery, centering users' shared narratives, manifesting as effortlessly swipeable feeds.

However, this insatiable user interaction currency has a dark side, giving rise to privacy and data monetization concerns. While we bask in the convenience and connectivity of these platforms, our personal data often becomes an exploitable commodity.

2.3. Social Media and Networking

Social media platforms essentially function as process facilitators, an aspect most evidently seen in networking. Connectivity allowed by these platforms surpasses the omnipresent 'social' categorization, extending to professional networking through portals like LinkedIn. Users can connect with potential employers, peers, and mentors, encouraging professional development and opportunities.

The impact isn't restricted to the individual; businesses utilize these platforms to engage consumers directly. This two-way communication promotes a consumer-oriented approach, with businesses capable of receiving instantaneous feedback and consumer insights.

2.4. Social Media and Digital Marketing

Social media's tremendous user base has attracted businesses, big and small alike, to use these platforms as marketing tools. Creating pages or handles on Facebook, Instagram, or Twitter allows businesses to expand their reach and directly communicate with their consumers.

Digital marketing on social media harnesses the power of analytics. Insight into users' interaction patterns and preferences ensures more effective, targeted advertising. Social media ads are not merely for visibility but for interaction, facilitating real-time consumer engagement.

While this has revolutionized marketing strategies, it also presents stringent ethical concerns about user data privacy and security.

2.5. Social Media and the Rise of Influencers

The essential facet of social media marketing is the rise of social media influencers. These individuals harness their established social media presence, characterized by substantial follower counts, to advocate or promote products, services, or even ideas.

Influencers have managed to establish an unprecedented humanization of the marketing process. The impact of an influencer's testimonial or review often surpasses traditional advertising, presenting a potent mix of reach and credibility.

However, the influencer industry is not immune to criticism, with issues such as transparency, authenticity, and the commodification of personal experiences drawing attention.

2.6. Social Media and its Societal Impact

Beyond connectivity and entertainment, social media has left an indelible mark on our social fabric. Its ability to disseminate information, organize movements, shape public opinions has fundamentally transformed our societal structure.

However, the barrage of information, sans reliable filtration mechanisms, has led to the proliferation of misinformation and fake news. Not to mention, it bears the potential to influence political processes and societal dynamics.

From propelling social movements like #MeToo or #BlackLivesMatter to amplifying political crises or humanitarian issues, social media's role in society is varied and complex.

2.7. The Challenges

Despite the serviceable assumptions and abundant benefits, traditional social media is riddled with challenges. Chief among these are issues pertaining to user data privacy, misinformation, and the rising toxicity of online interactions. The centralization of control and power in the hands of platform owners adds to these factors, making for an increasingly dystopic social media environment.

Deciphering these problems is instrumental for the transition towards a decentralized form of social media. It helps unravel the necessary tools and components that need transformation to usher in an era of responsible and libertarian online communication.

The exploration of traditional media sets the stage for understanding these fundamental challenges. Only by addressing them can we pave the new path towards a decentralized social media landscape empowered by blockchain technology.

While traditional social media has shaped our current digital landscape, its inherent flaws and limitations indicate the necessity of a new model. This model, predicated on decentralization, fairness, and data ownership, rests on leveraging technology like blockchain. Thus, understanding this traditional model is integral to appreciate and adapt to the potential future that decentralized social media interactions promise.

Chapter 3. Exploring the Concept of Decentralization

Decentralization, a concept often thrown about in various tech and economics circles, is at its core, a simple concept. It refers to the dispersal and distribution of functions, powers, people, or things away from a central location or authority.

While society has, for the most part, operated under centralized systems - be it governments, economic systems, or social organization structures - the tide is gradually shifting towards a decentralized model.

3.1. The Centralized vs. Decentralized Paradigm

To fully appreciate the concept, we first have to look at its counterpoint - centralization. In a centralized system, decision-making authority is concentrated at the top and information flows from one central point. It forms a hierarchy where every member reports up and receives instructions from the levels above. This model is prevalent in most governments, corporations, and societal institutions around the world.

However, centralization comes with its downsides. It can lead to an imbalance of power, bottleneck decision-making, reduce transparency, and create a single point of failure susceptible to attacks.

Decentralization, as you might have guessed, operates on a completely different logic. It is based on the principle of eliminating the need for a central authority by ensuring that power and decision-making capacity are distributed amongst all the members of the network.

In a decentralized system, no single entity has full control, but rather influence which is directly proportional to the role they play in maintaining the system. This plays a large role in forging a system that is transparent, resistant to censorship, and devoid of exploitation.

3.2. Decentralization in the Age of the Internet

The Internet was initially envisaged as a decentralized network, but with the advent of web servers, we saw a veer towards a somewhat centralized structure where information is sent from servers to clients (your computer, for instance). However, the last decade has seen a resurgence in the push for a decentralized Internet, and the driver behind this movement is blockchain technology.

Blockchain is a decentralized ledger that records transactions across multiple computers so that the record cannot be altered retroactively, without the alteration of all subsequent blocks. This enhances security and promotes transparency.

3.3. Understanding Peer to Peer Networks

One key aspect of decentralized systems is the 'peer-to-peer' (P2P) network model. A P2P network is a distributed architecture where individual nodes in the network (known as 'peers') share a part of their resources, such as processing power or network bandwidth, directly to other nodes without going through a central coordination point. This creates a network of equals where each node has the same privileges and each can initiate or complete a transaction.

P2P networks, when powered by cryptographic algorithms, form the foundation of blockchain implementations. Each peer has a copy of the entire blockchain and every transaction gets recorded into each peer's copy. If anyone attempts to alter a transaction, it will be rejected by other peers since it will not match their copy of the blockchain.

3.4. Evolution of Decentralized Platforms

With the capacity of blockchain technology understood, many platforms have started incorporating decentralization in their structures. For instance, Bitcoin - the popular cryptocurrency, is by far, one of the most entrenched implementations of this technology. It removed the need for a central bank to control money supply and instead, handed the control back to people, giving rise to the era of cryptocurrencies.

This evolution is not just confined to financial systems but has extended its reach to social media platforms as well. The idea of decentralized social media is to give users complete control over their data and work by introducing a democratic, user-driven model.

In conclusion, the shift towards decentralization has the potential to rewrite societal structures. By eliminating central points of control, we forge a society where people have more agency, businesses operate more transparently, and information flows more freely. Harnessing such a shift can lead to profound changes in how we, as a society, interact, communicate, and grow.

Chapter 4. The Mechanics of Blockchain Technology

Blockchain technology, arguably the backbone of decentralized social media, bares the complexity of a finely tuned and precision-engineered machine. It integrates areas of computer science and cutting-edge cryptography to deliver a decentralized, unalterable ledger system, which has the potential to affect several industries, primarily social media.

4.1. Understanding the Basics

To visualize blockchain as a system, think of it as an expanding chain of blocks. Each block contains a series of transactions and a unique identifier. The unique identifier, a cryptographic hash, not only labels the block but also links it to the preceding block. This link, formed via the cryptographic hash function, creates an unbroken chain that safeguards the integrity of the past transactions, making it a formidable tool against data tampering.

4.2. Components of a Blockchain: Blocks

A block contains a pointer to the hash of the last block, a timestamp, a list of transactions, and a nonce. The nonce is an arbitrary number that may only be used once. It's integral for the "Proof of Work" algorithm in blockchain. The block also records the transactions within that period. Typically, a new block is added around every ten minutes.

4.3. Cryptographic Hash Functions

Hash functions are one-way encryption algorithms used extensively in blockchain technology. A small change in the input radically changes the output, making it impossible to regenerate original data from the hash output. This assures a high level of security in the blockchain. The most common type of hash function used is SHA-256.

The hash function takes any input and gives a fixed size of alphanumeric string output. Regardless of the length, the input always yields a fixed 256-bits hash value when using SHA-256. This property is critical as even a small change in the transaction will result in a completely different hash, helping to quickly detect alterations to block details.

4.4. The Blockchain Ledger

The ledger is a full record of all blocks chained together from the genesis block (the first block) to the most recent one. It provides an exhaustive history of all transactions that have ever happened in the blockchain network.

A distributed ledger refers to the fact that this ledger isn't held in a central location but instead is stored across several nodes in the network. Each node has a copy of the whole ledger. This distribution brings about redundancy that leads to greater security and fault tolerance.

4.5. Decentralized Consensus

Blockchain technology has introduced novel ways of reaching consensus across a network of unequal trust—making it a cornerstone principle of decentralization. Two common mechanisms are Proof of Work (PoW) and Proof of Stake (PoS).

In the PoW consensus, the one to solve a complex mathematical problem first gets to add a block and is rewarded with a certain amount of cryptocurrency. It prevents any bad actor from controlling the network because it would require massive computational power.

It is worth noting that PoW can be energy-intensive, leading to the development of PoS. PoS chooses the creator of the new block based on their stake or amount of cryptocurrency they're willing to 'lock up' as a bet they're not trying to sabotage the system.

4.6. Smart Contracts

Smart contracts are self-executing contracts where the terms of an agreement are directly written into lines of code. These contracts leverage the decentralized nature of the blockchain to execute predefined rules without intermediaries.

Lifecycle of a smart contract includes creation, testing, and deployment. Once deployed, it becomes unalterable. A trigger generally initiates a smart contract, like a date or an event occurrence, and once started, it will undertake the role it's been designed for.

4.7. Forks in Blockchain

Forks are significant changes or upgrades to the protocols of the blockchain. They are characterized as either 'hard forks' or 'soft forks'. A hard fork is incompatible with the previous version, often leading to a split into two separate chains. A soft fork, however, is backward compatible, and users don't necessarily have to upgrade to continue using the system.

Forks are crucial in the evolution of the blockchain as they allow for errors to be corrected, developer community disagreements to be addressed, or new functionalities to be introduced.

4.8. Blockchain Advantages and Disadvantages

Blockchain technology provides decentralization, transparency, and security, enabling trustless peer-to-peer communication. However, the technology is still in its adolescence and faces issues like scalability, integration, legal, and environmental concerns, mainly due to the energy-intensive nature of the PoW consensus mechanism.

Blockchain technology is much more than just digital currency or payments. It's a new form of organizing, verifying, securing digital transactions and data. Its adoption in the realm of social media is still in nascent stages, and further chapters will unpack how this can shape the future of online communication.

Chapter 5. Guarding Privacy: The Core of Decentralized Social Media

Decentralization has always been at the heart of internet protocol design, emphasizing end-to-end communication where the core network path isn't the crucial determinant of communication. However, over the years, centralization in the form of gatekeepers has emerged, controlling data flow and subsequently, privacy.

5.1. Shifting Paradigm: Centralization to Decentralization

The proliferation of social media platforms has given these gatekeepers unprecedented access to personal data, exerting monopolistic control over information, often breaching the privacy sanctity people cherish. Decentralized Social Media (DSM), predicated online communication tools on blockchain technologies, promise a shift from this status quo. By decentralizing the control and returning the power back to users, DSM aims to guard privacy like never before.

5.2. Understand the Concept: How Decentralized Social Media Works

DSM operates on a peer-to-peer (P2P) network, which passes information directly between users rather than providing a centralized server to mediate communication. Here, each user doubles as a mini-server, rendering hierarchical structure and centralized control unnecessary. Blockchain technology underpins this approach, providing the backbone that maintains and verifies transaction records through consensus algorithms.

5.3. Privacy Protection: Cryptography and Blockchain

Cryptographic tools are integral to privacy protection in DSM. They use complex mathematical algorithms to secure information, rendering it unreadable to unauthorized users. Blockchain, the decentralized ledger, employs these algorithms in a way that maintains user anonymity while furnishing verifiable transaction records. Encryption and hash functions only allow users with the right decryption keys to access the information. Therefore, even if malicious actors intercept the communication, the information remains secure.

5.4. Decentralization and the Power of Anonymity

An essential feature of blockchain is the pseudonymity or quasi-anonymity it provides. While all transactions are transparent and verifiable on the blockchain network, user-identities need not be disclosed. This allows for a unique blend of accountability and privacy - you're responsible for your actions, but your identity remains obscured.

5.5. Real-world Application: Tor and the Power of Onion Routing

Tor, a free open-source software, offers insights into the practical applications of DSM. It uses onion routing to ensure privacy by encapsulating the data in multiple encryption layers. Each network node unpacks a single layer, which doesn't divulge the source, destination, and content in one go. This sophisticated process guarantees that no single entity can access complete information, thus safeguarding user privacy.

5.6. Limitations and Considerations: The Dark Side of Anonymity

While the promise of DSM and anonymity are exciting, it's vital to note the potential for misuse. Anonymity can be a double-edged sword: while it protects people's rights and freedoms, it can also create a breeding ground for illegal activities.

5.7. Overcoming Challenges: Reputation Systems and Regulations

Reputation systems can be a way forward, allowing users to rate and report based on behaviors, similar to traditional social media platforms. This adds an element of public accountability while protecting privacy, encouraging good behavior within the network.

Regulations can also play a significant role, setting rules and boundaries for the functioning of DSM. However, it poses challenges in terms of enforcement due to the lack of a central authority. Thus, regulation in the decentralized world needs a delicate balance, to safeguard privacy without infringing upon user autonomy.

5.8. Looking Forward: The Evolution of Decentralized Social Media

Blockchain technology and DSM are still evolving, presenting us with an opportunity to shape the technology and practices in a manner that emphasizes privacy. As the adage goes, 'with great power comes great responsibility.' As users and beneficiaries of DSM, it falls on our shoulders to responsibly and ethically uphold privacy standards.

In summary, DSM offers a fresh perspective to envision a world where privacy isn't sacrificed at the altar of convenience. While challenges and potential misuses exist, deliberate design choices and mindful usage can direct its evolution towards preserving privacy in the vibrant labyrinth of online interactions. The key lies in striking a balance between the endless possibilities that technology opens up and the principled path that circles back to the user – where it all started. A future is possible where we no longer have to trade privacy for connectivity - the core premise underpinning the grand vision of Decentralized Social Media.

Chapter 6. Advantages and Challenges of Decentralized Social Media

Online communication is at the dawn of a seismic shift, one that aims to unpick the entrenched issues current models face. Central to this momentous wave of change is Decentralized Social Media - a nexus of distributed ledger technology and social platforms that offers a vision of communication unshackled from the pitfalls of centralization. Decentralized Social Media comes with its suite of advantages and challenges, both of which will be deconstructed in extreme detail in the forthcoming sections.

6.1. Advantages of Decentralized Social Media

Decentralized Social Media, or DSM, leverages key features of blockchain technology to provide a plethora of advantages. These advantages range from enhancing user privacy and security to facilitating unprecedented levels of accountability.

6.2. Enhanced User Privacy

Traditional social media platforms control access to user-generated data, often leading to misuse, illegal data sharing, and advertising manipulations. In contrast, DSM (Decentralized Social Media) employs cryptographic functions underpinned by blockchain technology to provide secure, private, and personalized experiences to users. Each user possesses a unique private key, unavailable to anyone else on the network. This shield protects their information from unauthorized access, ensuring that the control, management, and privacy of data rests entirely with the user.

6.3. User Control and Profit Sharing

In the centralized model, the generated revenue from ads distributed across platforms lands primarily in the coffers of the platform owners, despite the content originating from users. DSM turns this profit model on its head. It enables users to have substantial control over ad preferences and revenue sharing. Coupled with the token economy, users can monetize their content and earn profit through mechanisms such as pay-per-view or contribution rewards.

6.4. Censorship-Resistance and Freedom of Speech

The peer-to-peer essence of DSM makes it inherently resistant to censorship. Unlike centralized systems where a single entity has the power to manipulate or restrict content visibility, DSM employs consensus algorithms to democratize decision-making power. Thus, content visibility and sharing become a product of collective agreement, fostering the true spirit of freedom of expression.

6.5. Greater Transparency and Accountability

Blockchains are immutable ledgers; every interaction on the network, once recorded, cannot be altered or tampered with. This immutability introduces a level of transparency and accountability unseen in traditional social media platforms, fortifying trust between users.

While the advantages paint an attractive picture, DSM is not without its complications and challenges.

6.6. Challenges of Decentralized Social Media

Many of the features that render DSM a powerful proposition for transformative social media platforms also introduce new and unique challenges. The hurdles range from scalability problems to the intricacies of managing an entirely new user control paradigm.

6.7. Technical Complexity and User Experience

Adopting DSM implies getting familiar with a suite of blockchain-related concepts. Private keys, cryptography, smart contracts, tokens - the learning curve is steep and may be a tough pill for non-technical users to swallow. The user experience (UX) must prioritize simplicity to adopt broader usage.

6.8. Scalability

As the blockchain operates on a peer-to-peer network, its capacity for data transaction remains limited. As more users start to engage, platforms may struggle to process transactions quickly and efficiently. Improved consensus algorithms and off-chain solutions are potential remedies but require significant research and development.

6.9. Legal and Regulatory Concerns

In the nascent stage, the legal and regulatory framework around DSM is in flux. User anonymity can lead to illegal practices, including hate speech or dissemination of harmful content, muddying the waters for law enforcement. We need robust, adaptable laws for governing DSM.

6.10. Misinformation and False Narratives

Decentralization advocates for freedom of speech, but this advantage can be a two-edged sword. It can foster proliferation of false information or harmful narratives due to lack of centralized moderation, resulting in a misinformed user base or facilitating malevolent activities.

In conclusion, the architecture of Decentralized Social Media provides compelling arguments in favor of more open, user-centric social platforms. However, the path towards implementing such platforms isn't without friction, and the solutions to these challenges require a delicate balance between preserving user rights and ensuring societal harmony.

Chapter 7. Behind the Scenes: How Blockchain Drives Decentralized Platforms

In the world of technology, few innovations have stirred as much intrigue as blockchain. Initially established as the driving force behind cryptocurrencies like Bitcoin, blockchain technology has come a long way. One of its most promising uses lies in powering decentralized platforms, including social media.

7.1. Understanding Blockchain

To understand how blockchain drives decentralized platforms, we must first establish what a blockchain is. A blockchain is essentially a digital ledger, where information is stored across various computers in multiple locations. Each block in the chain contains a number of transactions, and every time a new transaction occurs on the blockchain, a record of that transaction is added to every participant's ledger, making it near-impossible to tamper with.

The decentralization provided by blockchain is revolutionary. No single individual or organization has control over the entire blockchain, and each participant, or 'node,' has access to a complete copy of the ledger. This differs dramatically from traditional, centralized databases, accessible only by their owners.

7.2. The Mechanism of Decentralization

Blockchain's decentralized nature brings about transparency, security, and freedom from intermediary controls. In contrast to centralized platforms controlled by single entities, decentralized platforms relying on blockchain technology allow peer-to-peer interaction. Let's delve into how this happens.

Blockchain attributions such as hashed time-stamping and cryptographic security pave the way for secure, verifiable transactions. Transactions on a blockchain are bundled into blocks, which are sealed using complex mathematical problems. Miners, specialized nodes within the blockchain, work to solve these problems. The first miner to solve it adds the new block to the chain, making the transaction information within immutable.

7.3. Blockchain Consensus Algorithms

For a decentralized platform to function, its nodes need to agree on the state of the shared ledger. This agreement process is guided by consensus algorithms. The two most renowned are Proof of Work (PoW) and Proof of Stake (PoS).

PoW, used by Bitcoin, involves miners solving mathematical puzzles. The power and resources used give 'proof of work,' validating the transaction. PoS, on the other hand, allows node validators to create new blocks based on the amount of digital currency they hold and are willing to 'stake' for the validation process. Both methods serve to deter faulty transactions.

7.4. Implementing Blockchain in Decentralized Social Media

Translating these concepts into social media evokes the idea of platforms where no control is held by a single entity, and content moderation and data privacy are community-handled. By being part of a decentralized social media platform, users could potentially take control of their content, keeping it safe from censorship or misuse.

Blockchain brings trustworthiness to a decentralized social media platform. Every post, like, comment – every interaction becomes a transaction stored on the blockchain. As transactions are irreversible and time-stamped, content cannot be altered unnoticed. This maintains the integrity of the information and the accountability of the users.

7.5. Challenges and Potential

Despite the promise, challenges abound. For decentralized social media platforms to gain widespread acceptance, issues surrounding user experience, scalability, and legal implications must be addressed. Blockchain technology, while revolutionary, is complex and demands considerable resources, which could limit scalability aspects.

The potential, however, is immense. Decentralized social media could disrupt the paradigm of data privacy and control, returning the power to the users. As we stand on the precipice of this digital revolution, the exciting mystery is not if these changes will happen – it's when, and how profoundly they will reshape our digital interactions.

With these concepts in mind, it is clear that blockchain technology lies at the beating heart of the next generation of decentralized platforms. Understanding this complex technology is key to unlocking the potential of a future where digital freedom, privacy, and democratization are not just idealistic dreams, but tangible realities.

Chapter 8. Case Studies: Existing Decentralized Social Networks

There are various decentralized social networks that serve as intriguing case studies on the advent of this newfound technology. Each signifies the stepping stones towards a more independent and secure approach to online communication.

8.1. Steemit: Social Media on the Blockchain

Steemit, a blockchain-based blogging and social media platform, offers tokens to its content creators and curators. Built on the Steem Blockchain, it uses a novel mechanism for rewarding users - Steem tokens, which can be exchanged for other cryptocurrencies or fiat currency.

Steemit's blockchain also produces blocks every 3 seconds. By implementing the delegated Proof of Stake (dPoS) consensus algorithm, witnesses (block producers) are elected by token holders, creating a democratic layer over mining. One notable feature is the ability to perform transactions without fees, as blockchain covers costs by inflation.

Despite criticism for excessive rewards to early adopters, Steemit showcased the perks of combining social media and blockchain. It gave content creators the chance to reap financial benefits directly, a stark difference from traditional social networks that extract the economic value they generate.

8.2. Mastodon: A Twitter Alternative with Decentralization

Mastodon is a decentralized social network established as an alternative to Twitter. Differently from prevailing social platforms, it deploys a federated model, allowing users to run and administer their server instances while communicating with others on different servers.

Through this method, Mastodon relinquishes control to users, providing a participatory governance model. Like other open-source projects, volunteers maintain its codebase and users propose features directly. Its purpose is to avoid single points of failure and promote user control and customizability.

Notably, each Mastodon server, or "instance," applies its moderation policies. This delegation empowers users, ensuring they are part of an environment aligned with their preferences, and mitigates against centralized algorithmic control and censorship.

8.3. Diaspora: The User-owned, Privacy-centric Network

Diaspora represents one of the early attempts at a decentralized social network. Created as a reaction to privacy concerns over Facebook, it adopted a unique distributed model named "pods." Users either select a pod hosted by someone else or self-host, providing a stark contrast to centralized data collection models.

Data on Diaspora is owned by users, meaning the platform itself does not sell or misuse personal information. It allows users to utilize pseudonyms for account creation, championing online privacy.

Diaspora's case demonstrates the feasibility of privacy-centric, user-owned networks. However, due to its low adoption rate and technical barriers (such as setting up pods), it underscores the difficulties faced by decentralized social media platforms in achieving wide-scale user adoption.

8.4. Blockstack: DApps and a New Internet

Blockstack is not merely a decentralized social network but an ecosystem for decentralized applications (DApps). It proposes a new internet where personal data resides with the user, and applications run on user devices.

Blockstack's Browser enables access to DApps. Users authenticate using an identity anchor and, afterward, interact with DApps, storing any application data directly. Data storage, named Gaia, decentralizes the storage of user data, leveraging existing private storage systems.

This case presents a bold vision, illustrating the next generation of social media might arise from ecosystems, not independent platforms. Yet, hurdles persist - achieving scalability, interoperability, and user-friendliness remain key challenges.

8.5. Other noteworthy mentions

Mind, Sola, and Manyverse are other decentralized social networks of note. Each has pioneered with unique features and models, contributing to the nascent decentralized social media landscape. Yet, they also underline core challenges, such as user adoption, monetization, and scalability.

Overall, the examples above indicate numerous directions for the evolution of decentralized social media. Each network has its strength and weakness, and it's clear there is no one-size-fits-all model. As we delved into these case studies, the overarching themes revolved around user control, data privacy, monetization, and user-friendly experiences, offering instructive cues for the future of decentralized social media.

Chapter 9. Navigating the Regulatory Landscape

The era of Decentralized Social Media (DSM) heralds a vast sea of possibilities, teeming with numerous advantages like enhanced security, privacy, and user control. However, the entire ecosystem floats amidst a complex regulatory environment, making it crucial for all stakeholders to tread cautiously while pushing boundaries.

9.1. Navigating Regulatory Complexities

Decentralized systems revamp the traditional platform-user dynamics, giving rise to myriad legal and regulatory challenges. Regulating such decentralized systems, which operate across various jurisdictions, is difficult due to the absence of a central authority. Therefore, the regulatory focus tends to shift towards users who participate in maintaining the DSM network by running nodes or validating transactions.

For instance, content moderation, a typical responsibility of centralized platform providers, becomes challenging in a decentralized setup. While the system may prevent third-party data manipulation, it also elevates the risks of dissemination of illicit content.

Moreover, the diversified, global user-base of the DSM further complicates regulatory oversight. Several nations are moving towards legislating the digital realm. However, widespread disagreements concerning the definition and valuation of online rights, responsibilities, and restrictions continue to pose hindrances.

9.2. The Data Protection Conundrum

One of the crucial aspects of DSM regulation is data protection. The European Union's General Data Protection Regulation (GDPR), for example, emphasizes user consent, data portability, data minimization, and rights to be forgotten. However, complying with these principles is challenging for DSMs due to their immutable nature and privacy features. For instance, the right to be forgotten is almost impossible to guarantee in a setup where data is permanently engraved on a chain of blocks.

Encryption technologies used in DSM can potentially clash with law enforcement and government surveillance efforts. Similar to the 'going dark' problem, where investigators cannot access encrypted data even with a court order, regulators can find it hard to access encrypted communications on DSM platforms.

9.3. Deciphering Ownership and Intellectual Property

With a DSM, numerous entities are contributing to the network's maintenance and content dissemination. As a result, determining accountability and ownership becomes complex, significantly impacting regulations related to intellectual property and copyrights. These challenges necessitate the evolution of existing legal systems to foster proper ownership attribution and enforcement mechanisms in a decentralized world.

9.4. The Cross-Border Challenge

DSMs are typically borderless, functioning seamlessly across geographical limitations. This is both an advantage and a headache for regulators. The absence of geo-restrictions means that DSMs can provide unprecedented freedom of speech and expression. At the same time, they make it difficult to apply country-specific laws.

International cooperation becomes a pressing need in this context, as DSM regulatory frameworks require being globally agreed upon, adopted, and enforced. However, the process is convoluted due to varied legal frameworks, political systems, and cultural values across nations. Countries will have to collaborate to build an internationally harmonized regulatory system that respects sovereignty while facilitating seamless cross-border digital interactions.

9.5. Blockchain Regulations

As the underlying technology of DSM, understanding blockchain regulations is vital in this pursuit. Some territories, such as China, have adopted a stringent stance on blockchain, frequently fluctuating between allowing blockchain development while curbing cryptocurrency usage. In contrast, others like Switzerland have open regulatory environments welcoming blockchain innovation.

Regulating blockchain becomes complicated due to its unique nature; it associates with both financial transactions (cryptocurrencies) and non-financial data (blockchain-based applications). The duality makes it susceptible to a wide array of regulatory frameworks, often straddling areas like financial law and telecommunications.

Understanding and navigating the regulatory landscape of DSM require concerted efforts from policymakers, technologists, and users alike. Building an inclusive DSM ecosystem calls for flexibility to change, willingness for global cooperation, and embracing the concept of decentralized platforms. The path might be arduous and intertwined, but the potential rewards - a borderless, decentralized platform respecting user privacy and control - are incredibly enticing and undoubtedly worth the journey.

Chapter 10. The Economic Impact of Decentralized Social Media

It's no secret that the global economy is transitioning towards a digital model. This transformation is bolstered by the rise of advanced technologies such as Artificial Intelligence (AI), Internet of Things (IoT), and blockchain. In this paradigm shift, an exciting new system is coming of age - decentralized social media. Reflecting the key attributes of blockchain technology, such as decentralization, immutability, and transparency, this innovation is poised to considerably influence the economic landscape.

10.1. Impact on Advertising Revenue Model

A critical area of revolution, courtesy of decentralized social media, is the advertising sector. Traditional social media platforms function on a centralized model, where they collect, control, and exploit user data for their monetary gain through targeted ads. In stark contrast, decentralized platforms give back this control to users who can choose to not disclose their data or to monetize it.

This shift is not merely a blow to the monopolistic domination of tech giants over user data but also paves the way towards a democratized ad revenue model. Users, content creators, and advertisers can engage in direct transactions, potentially boosting the effectiveness and efficiency of marketing campaigns. Less revenue leakage in the advertising ecosystem means more profits for stakeholders involved.

10.2. Empowering Individuals

Decentralized social media, breaking away from traditional data acquisitory practices, empower users to own their digital identity. Users on these platforms decide what part of their data is for public consumption, including the ability to monetize it. The social media economy can thus transform into a contributory model, not merely confined to content creation but extended to data contribution. This change can lead to an uptick in global online spending patterns and influence global economic indicators.

10.3. Tokenization of Digital Assets

Blockchain technology, an integral part of the decentralized model, has introduced a remarkable concept - tokenization. While cryptocurrencies like Bitcoin are the most famous tokens, the process can extend to any digital and physical assets, turning them into tradeable commodities on the platform. Decentralized social platforms can leverage this mechanism, converting "likes," "shares," and "comments" into values that hold real-world significance. This conversion can lead to a parallel economy, rooted in user engagement and digital interaction.

10.4. Job Market Transformation

The decentralized social media model has the potential to transform the job market significantly. Given its transparent and immutable nature, blockchain can validate identities, experiences, and skills, creating a trustless environment where users can interact, collaborate, and transact. This new paradigm can support the gig economy and freelance workspaces—creating a borderless work ecosystem, allowing for the creation of jobs and financial independence for a broader audience.

10.5. The Future of E-commerce

The confluence of decentralized social media and e-commerce could reimagine online shopping experiences. Blockchain technology can inject transparency, data security, and user control– aspects that have become increasingly important for consumers. This amalgamation enables users to shop directly from social media platforms, dramatically reducing transaction fees that traditional middlemen or payment gateways would charge, thereby affecting global e-commerce trends.

In conclusion, the advent of decentralized social media, grounded on the principles of user-centric control and transparent operations, promises to reshape the global economic taxonomy. From democratizing the advertising revenue model to empowering individuals, tokenization of digital assets, transforming the job market, and the future of e-commerce - the economic repercussions of this innovation are manifold and magnanimous. As we steer into this future, the challenge lies in ensuring that this shift is regulated and secure, maintaining the balance between innovation and safety. The dawn of this new era certainly symbolizes an exciting journey, ripe with opportunities, and a page waiting to be written in our economic history.

Chapter 11. Envisioning the Future: The Global Impact of Decentralized Social Media

Decentralized Social Media (DSM) is not merely a technological innovation; it has the potential to reshape the societal fabric on a global scale. Its ramifications for freedom, economics, politics, and social interconnectivity are profound, implicating new ways to participate not only in digital environments but in our shared global community. To envision the future shaped by decentralized social media, one must understand DSM's core principles, examine its potential for global influence, and scrutinize any threats or challenges that it might face.

11.1. Understanding the Core Principles of Decentralized Social Media

DSM operates on a range of scalable, decentralized technologies, chief among them being blockchain. The principle underpinning these technologies involves dissolving central points of control to promote user autonomy. In the context of social media, this means enabling individuals to become the true owners of their digital identities, expressions, and data.

Blockchain adoption in DSM assigns unique digital identities to users. It's connectively intertwining with other networks, creating immutable and publicly verifiable records of online activities. A vital feature of DSM is the inherent prevention of unauthorized access, imposing a significant barrier on data misuse.

By decentralizing data storage, the risk of single-point failures is minimized. Each user's data can be stored encrypted, retrieved, and validated using cryptographic mechanisms specific to the individual. This setup ensures that users retain complete control over their digital presence, from the data they generate to the interactions they undertake.

11.2. Prospective Global Impact of DSM

The real-world implications of DSM are diverse and far-reaching.

11.2.1. Freedom and Individual Rights

DSM has the potential to impact significant areas of individual rights and freedom. With DSM, the power in digital communication shifts from corporations back to individuals. Users can choose how they want to interact, who can access their data, and manage their digital rights.

As the chorus for online privacy grows louder, DSM could safeguard individuals against unwarranted surveillance, whether by corporations, advertisers, or governments. With more control over personal data, users will be better equipped to protect their digital footprints.

11.2.2. Economic Facets

DSM's economic influence stems from its capability to directly monetize user interactions. It could lead to a new digital economy where users are rewarded for contributions - a significant change from the current model where profits are concentrated within a few dominant players.

Additionally, with data being valuable assets, DSM could facilitate decentralized marketplaces for consensually shared data. Users could monetize their data, imbuing the data trade with a more equitable distribution of wealth.

11.2.3. Governance and Politics

DSM interfaces could be used to extend digital, decentralized, and verifiable systems of voting, thereby fostering greater transparency and voter turnout in political systems worldwide. This shift could result in more representative governance, reducing the scope for corruption and enhancing political participation.

11.3. Potential Threats and Challenges to DSM Adoption

Despite the anticipated benefits, the path towards DSM adoption is strewn with significant challenges and threats.

11.3.1. Technological Hurdles

While the potential for scalable DSM platforms hinges on blockchain and decentralized web technologies, these are still in nascent stages. Achieving a user-friendly, scalable, and reliable DSM platform would require significant technological advancements.

11.3.2. Regulation and Legal Challenges

DSM's decentralized nature poses challenges to the current regulatory and legal landscape. As DSM operates on a transnational scale, it raises issues regarding jurisdiction and enforcement of laws, which would require cooperation and consensus among diverse international stakeholders.

11.3.3. Adoption Challenge

A significant challenge is driving large-scale adoption. Users accustomed to centralized platforms may resist the transition to DSM due to the learning curve involved. Overcoming this barrier would require conscious effort to educate the populace regarding the benefits of DSM.

In conclusion, the prospective global impact of Decentralized Social Media is immense and game-changing. However, actualizing this vision would require concerted efforts across technological development, regulatory redesign, and individual adaptability. As we steadily progress toward this era of decentralized digital communication, a new horizon of individual rights, economic equitability, and transparent governance holds the promise of becoming reality. The potential benefits of DSM clearly outweigh the challenges, marking it as a significant player in shaping our digital future.